A Tribute to
The African Child

Rabiu Momoh

Dedication

This book is dedicated to every African child in the world. All that you are and all that you've seen remains just a tiny piece of what can be. Reach within, find that spark and make our world better than what it is. You are loved. You are strong. Keep being the very best of you.

Acknowledgments

My sincere appreciation to all the inspiring figures in my life, most especially my lovely wife, Jumoke Momoh, and my beautiful daughter, Temiloluwa Momoh. You both give more than what can be told in words. My sincere thanks to the Momohs and the Buraimohs far and near. Your support sets in motion everything good. To the CMUL YBC '09 crew and all the other wonderful souls, friends and colleagues, who have shaped experiences and contributed to my journey, may our sweet interactions never end. God will always continue to deserve the most praise in our lives.

Poem Topics

1.

Tribute to The African Child

Such was his spirit,
When everything conspired to make timid
In a world that answers no by default
What he would become who knows
Each day, ever stoking the fire for the day's fight
When conquering each day is more than required
Toiling blood, sweat and tears became like a birthright
The hot afternoon sun never made the journey light
Like a tortoise within its shell, it feels like I'm really stuck here

The hopes of a better tomorrow
Daily wishing to live easier with lesser sorrows
The survival fight cuts deep to the marrow
Stark realities of a life that looks borrowed
Bearing the pain around like a spiritual halo
Oh, that hollow that often blights my soul
That nothingness that makes me want to growl.
Oh, my soul why doth thou feel this low
Like an ant on a mission to the end of the world,
My journey really feels so long

How my spirit desires to rise and fly
Truly fly in the sky so high; I guess I might
Fly above the zillion stakes ever raised so high
Far from my detractors and those that might
Like tattoos etched upon skin, I bear my plights

Setting lights to the skies of my darkest nights.
Bearing the emblems of my small victories like the Queen's knights,
Like a maiden found her lover, my joy blows over

The hopes of better days truly beckon
The sacrifices to be paid each day I must reckon
Keeping my feet firm on the grounds that I walk on
Still keeping the faith till my fights are won
And the joy in my heart knowing no limits like a spaceship set sail.

Rabiu Momoh

2.

Admonition (The Medley)

These were the words of my father;
Attend to my words, son, and honour your mother
Many who haven't, have gone from Prada to Nada.
I have forged my own path with Dreams from My Father.
You would find all the love you can get in Hamlet
Cherish the friendship you have in Romeo and Juliet
Please remember our lessons from the Animal Farm
The Audacity of Hope will take you far
There would be few Avengers fighting your cause in the city
Between home and yonder, you'd have learnt A Tale of Two Cities
You'd learn to always stand on your feet
Everyone there learns the Art of the Deal
You might find yourself working for the Merchant of Venice
You might work in King Solomon's Mines
But never stop to Think Big and deal with Gifted Hands
Some nights are beautiful as the One Thousand and One Arabian
    Nights
Giving you thrills better than Alice in Wonderland
Some other nights are full of Tempests
Feeling like it's Much Ado About Nothing and Things Fall Apart
Weep not Child,
Be a Survivor like the Destiny's Child
Ensure they only bring out your best
For when the Arrow of God strikes,
the gods are not to blame
In all you face, always look for the Endgame

Sometimes it's Mo' Money, Mo' Problems
You'd have seen life in 50 Shades of Grey talking to your own children
Others would have seen it 50 Shades Darker
When you fall, you'll need the Art of the Comeback
Learn all you can from Anthony and Cleopatra
Like my friend David Copperfield,
you don't always have to Kill a Mockingbird
Ensure you never have A Time to Kill
Some days would feel longer than Mandela's Long Walk to Freedom
Let them remind you where you have come from
Days of Our Lives would be there for you to watch
Don't get in the path of the Runaway Bride
Learn from Pride and Prejudice
You'll see the vicissitudes of life like Gulliver's Travels
Don't play the Devil's Advocate
Stay far from hate
When you find Mary Jane,
put a Purple Hibiscus in her hair
In your life's quest, remember the story in Macbeth.

Rabiu Momoh

3.

My Immortal

Cheers to my Lady in Red
Your Uptown Funk and Finesse stand all beyond compare
I hope you stay Forever Young
With the boys gazing, I know I am Not the Only One
Sometimes I'm Speechless like I Took a Pill in Ibiza
Sometimes Love-stoned and staring into Blank Space
With you, I'd wish an Adventure of a Lifetime
When you pass by, you give thrills Time After Time
Your sweet words are like Drops of Jupiter
Just gazing at you is as beautiful as Counting Stars
Hey Soul Sister, your love keeps forever giving
We will never be in a Bad Romance
Oh, I wish you'd Save Me the Last Dance tonight,
You'd never know Where Broken Hearts Go

Ours would be an Endless Love
On your coldest nights, I will Set Fire to The Rain
Through the downpours, I will Make it Through the Rain
In our ocean of love, we'll sail from Coast to Coast
To us, I'll forever make a toast
You'll find me stronger than a Dark Horse
Like 03 Bonny and Clyde, there'll be no stopping us
Stay With Me even if the Skyfalls
To the Ones That Got Away, We're Never Getting Back Together Billy
    Jean's got 99 Problems, Angelica and her sugar fathers
In the forest of Deborah's love, I'll have enough to gather
You're my Immortal, Debby.

Rabiu Momoh

5

4.

The Reunion

It feels like yesterday when we all parted
Like memories of times spent together would never be re-enacted
But time has given a second chance
Oh, What I would give for another dance with Lisa
Some of the best souls I've met are with you, my colleagues
Looks like they don't make breeds of your league anymore
Days leading up to today weren't without a lot of anticipation
Thanks to individuals who have made it here across nations
Here would always feel like home, no matter how far I roam

Some things have remained the same,
like they were ten years ago
Nate has remained the same ever-animated fellow
Exuding so much life,
the fall of which we may never know
Oriyo has remained untouched in natural beauty
May you be forever framed,
framed in the gallery of things for infinity
As expected, Kel has lived in all the world's continents
What's left is a remembrance of your giftedness in a monument

Cheers to the love stories that have stood the tests of time
Turning a simple friendly meeting into something sublime
To Chloe and Tru,
To one another please remain ever true
In the race for baldness,

Joe leads the pack with so much calmness and boldness
With arid scalp greeting sunshine with so much openness
May your reign be without end
Nolan has populated the earth far more than anyone can count over
May your manliness live forever

Some moments stay fresh in memory
The many prom nights in all their fashion glory
The bonfires and their endless stories
The many Halloweens and all their shades of scary
To the many Valentines and the breakups after
To our famous college dropout turned millionaire,
Your ingenuity seems to beat what many seek after

To the homies and ladies that we lost
Your images tell us one could live forever young
Bearing your honour on is something that we must
To our colleagues in service of the nation,
May your happiness be without portion
My love to those who couldn't be here
May we all find peace and happiness in all that we dare
Cheers to another beautiful 10 years.

Rabiu Momoh

5.

Point of no return

Beyond that door, Papa, everything changes
An exit leading to points unknown
What lies beyond remains an utmost mystery
An utmost riddle to which I may one day fall
Happening by lure, force or exchange,
for most, the journey began so
Those who left have never been back
Leaving in the prime of youth
Memories around here never to be made again
A loss to this ground, a gain to points unknown
Beyond this door, dreams may be broken
Tales beyond this door stay mostly unspoken
Many a worth in exchange for a token
Many the motherland's dreams ultimately but lost
A libation to those who have gone before
I hope the future holds good in store
We hope someday you'll return to land once adored
More than a marvel, we know not who's next
But the thing surely goes around
Turn by turn, the best of us bid goodbye
Papa, beyond that door is a point of no return.

6.

The Close Shave

Some called it fate
Like we fell for the devil's bait
Events leading on at a fast rate
As though punishment out to those without faith
Like we led tops among sinners being weighed
Unplanned visitors knocking on heaven's gate
I had a close shave

Someone lock up the graves
The night the deep wouldn't regard the brave
A welcome evening for anyone including the depraved
With the Princes of this world going on a rave,
Girl sought refuge in the farthest cave
Others in the deep forest ends to be saved
Without a magical wand to wave
Dave, I had a close shave

Quietness and lull gave way to fracas
Francisca, Helena, Rasheeda and Franca
All wishing for a saviour in their mothers
Rents of shouts and cries blended in the open air
Far heart-rending to be measured in octaves
Expecting any help, they soon couldn't bother
Mother, I had a close shave

They say we'll need more than good luck to bring back the girls
Oh, mothers, your dear girls left their suck
Everyone looked to pass on the buck
Their exodus to Sambisa no one could block
Bus by bus, they arrived neverland in a flock
On what felt like judgement day,
Father, I had a close shave.

Dedicated to The Chibok Girls

Rabiu Momoh

Excerpt from "A Tribute To The African Child"

"How my spirit desires to rise and fly
Truly fly in the sky so high; I guess I might
Fly above the zillion stakes ever raised so high
Far from my detractors and those that might
Like tattoos etched upon skin, I bear my plights
Setting lights to the skies of my darkest nights
Bearing the emblems of my small victories like the Queen's knights
Like a maiden found her lover, my joy blows over"

7.

The Parturient

Deep inside, I felt the sign of life
Parts shaping out without a sculptor's knife
Cell upon cell, all laid out without a strife
Foretold stories of the fate of a future wife
Deep mysteries unfolding right before the world's eyes
Girlish curves lost to a wonderful gain
Product of an ancient process of conception
Sweet juice bathing a waiting sister to hallowed ascension

Oh Mama, never thought for this, I could have been trained
Hips broadened to receive a welcome weight
Face botched out fat, flouting every call to wait
Breasts to Jupiter's size, a food basket to create
Inward and outward changes, a new life was sustained
Cain, all attempts to feign the changes were in vain
Carried like a precious cargo in the world's eye, ever gingerly till due date

And then came the forces of contractions
Far beyond any form of helpful assumption
You'd see a show of blood, Mama said
And then it's only the beginning of everything good
Wave after wave came the unimaginable pain
Then came the McCain, the pain doctor, to save the day
Taking all the pain away with his magic chirocaine
Cain, blessed are you among children

Your bag of water showed ripened below like the full moon
And then there was a gush of your liquor faster than soon
Boom! The irrepressible urge to push
You crowned like Julius Caesar in full glory
And the rest of the actions were no story
The skies of my spirit rented at your first cry
With us, you'd only have to just try
You are the child of my youth, Cain
And our friendship has only just begun.

Rabiu Momoh

8.

A Letter to My Brother

Dear Casper,
When did we grow apart, the dear son of my mother?
I hope it's all added up in times so far
Your dreams, your drive and your loving manners
Your charisma, mixed with beautiful enigma
Your effortless soulfulness that leaves everyone in awe and cheerful
    wonder
All of those, I hope life hasn't smothered
Early enough, in you found an assumed leader
Taking the stakes so I'll need no minder
Running the playgrounds in the heat of the southern sun
Other memories were as refreshing as the summer rain
How we would sit to those memorable suppers
Rocking the town in our pride shoes made of rubber
Those long walks with your lovely dog, Glover
I was least prepared for your dream exit to countries yonder
At passing thoughts of you, I reflexly would shudder
At other times, I would beam in smiles knowing you couldn't be any
    better

Lovely brother, the first seed of my father
Wherever you are, I hope life treats you fairer
I hope you find more lift in your wings to fly higher
What you've become really, I often would ponder
Hope you'll return to us someday,
someday with your quiver full of more wonders

Our little sister Florica still stutters
I found a soulmate in Clarissa
Glover left us with 3 puppies, Boxer, Lister and Charitha
Find me brother, your true blood,
Dexter.

Rabiu Momoh

9.

The Fallen Soldier

It took a moment and a shot
And my blood goes wetting the enemy's ground
Laying there next to my friend upon the sands
Life slowly draining out, clutching at any remaining strand
Thinking, upon this land, again, I'll never stand
Fighting the honour of my King,
I've given all that's demanded
With all dutifulness, I've led my command
While you bawl, please remember me.

And there I laid,
Drained in strength never to rise again
Memories flashing through, while the soul prayed
The sun blazing down its heat, with nothing for shade
Far and near goes gunshot and sounds of grenades
Your will I've obeyed, never to have my lemonade
End of life, feeling a stumble through an empty long colonnade
My time stops soon, please remember me

To my lovely Adeline and my boy Harold,
Today's outcome was never foretold
You've always known the world can be so cold
So please, always ensure your fold
Through Harold's dream search for gold, Adeline,
His loving hands, forever please don't lose hold
Teach his occasional feeble hands to make bold
You'll find a new love Adeline, please remember me

My time fades away, I hope someone tells my story
The pushes, the barges, the fights and many nights of glory
One battle lost but many nights of victories
To this life of pain and joy, I've been a signatory
To my fellow soldiers, please ensure the territories
My mind pens this letter and it's all valedictory
My time stops now, but the earth remains
Please remember me.

Rabiu Momoh

10.

Rotimi

Dear Mother Whale,
I hope my tale is told as blood washes offshore
Beyond home and down to this clime, nothing is assured
Next to Mother Atlantic, I really should have found succour
There I laid by the coast, a free meal like nothing ever seen before
A toast to those needing meat, a meal for now and one for the store
Basket after basket, I was served out to happy boasts
Like one to perdition, blow after blow I was gored
Every bit of me making for food, nothing stood a flaw
To the young ones - knife in hand,
to the old - chainsaw was required

Dear Mother, I can only describe in words what I saw
My pain and experience should never be felt for sure
I laid victim to a nation with unenforced waterlines
A bloody afternoon by all descriptions, I met no salvation
Like one to damnation, I was welcomed in a weird ovation
To all and sundry, I stood a wonderful food ration
Dear Mother Whale, tell the herd not to swim this way
At this bay, there would be nothing left to say

Dear Mother,
I thought we were the pride of the sea, one to be conserved
An endangered species, one to be preserved
In the hands of my captors, I met an ill-reserved fate
One never to happen again by any order or date

Tell the gatekeepers about these dudes, their ways to change
I'm left with memories of times with the boys
And how in the bodies of waters we'd joyfully range
My love to the community of whales
Your lovely son,

Rotimi.

Rabiu Olusola Momoh

11.

Letter to My Daughter's Teacher

Dear Felicia,
I pen you words from the heart of a loving father
Please find an untouched soul in my daughter, Isabella
Mind so pure, divine and ever eager
Eager to engage the world around her without a bother
When everyone today jealously guards borders
Her spirit reminds me what we once were
Each day, her vigour renewed, I play catchers
Through life's murky waters,
Please teach her to remain a dreamer

A dreamer
A believer
Those her qualities that would take her further
Help her realise that today, the stakes are ever higher
That the odds would often be against her
Ever teach her, for her dreams, to remain a fighter
Not to go through life playing watchers
The rich getting richer and the poor poorer
That this decision would be forever hers
Like an archer, she should always set mind to purpose
She must mean what she says
And say what she means
Teach her to stay in school
But be a student of life
Teach her not to strife with all men

Life,
Teach her that this life is a journey
A journey, a journey with many turnings
She'll learn to hit the ground running
When she falls, she should never remain on her knees
Never be given to making pleas and excuses
Through life's school, she must be ready to pay the fees
While finding everything else,
She must be prepared to find herself.

Rabiu Momoh

12.

The Fallen Star

Standing there in the Heavens in all enviable sight
Next to the all-in-all, a symbol of light
Donned in purity, apparel shining so bright
Light so bright, downing every shade of night
Excellence personified, you had no need for a fight
Bearing the King's rule, you exude so much might
With spirit standing forthright and upright,
You were our morning star

To your excellence, all things stood in order
Over the formless earth, with you, we'd gleefully hover
All mysteries, at your consultation, stood but deciphered
To you we'd defer
To you we'd refer
Soon, your worship was all we could consider
You were our bringer of light

Fallen,
Fallen so far and so hard
Still falling with nothing to break the plunge
Far from the Heavens and any hope of recalling
You sinned, rubbing shoulders with the Father of Light
You are Lucifer, the son of the light
And you fell from grace.

Rabiu Momoh

Excerpt from "The Fallen Soldier"

"My time fades away; I hope someone tells my story
The pushes, the barges, the fights, and many nights of glory
One battle lost but many nights of victories
To this life of pain and joy, I've been a signatory
To my fellow soldiers, please ensure the territories
My mind pens this letter and it's all valedictory
My time stops now, but the earth remains
Please remember me."

13.

The Drama at Asystole

Mortals quick to displace thoughts of the 'endless hole'
Moment feeling far, but remains ultimately foretold
Spirit and soul, eternity forever taking hold
Life spilling out like water out of a bowl
The human essence from its corpus to infinity forever doled
Life roles and failures played out in a quick scroll, out of control
A loss to everything that makes a man whole
A journey to agelessness without an option of parole
There remains a drama at asystole

Drama! The ultimate drama!
Happening daily from Alabama to Addis Ababa
From Parma to Maitama, everyone's a comer to the drama
To some from trauma, to others from karma
To some is given a chance at melodrama
To some, the child remains taken from Mama
Like seed cast to ground in the hand of the farmer
There remains a solo drama at asystole

Sounds to fade from beep, beeeep, and beeeeeep.
Like a fade from the world plunging into the deep
Far in the distance went the doctors' bleeps
One on top chest might take a leap and do some flips
Hoping to stop a soul from humanity to eternally seep
Meds through veins pushed fast or running in drips
Across the room, loved ones would weep

Other times just strong enough to take a peep
Just before that trip, there remains a drama at asystole

To every man, there remains this test
The end of the survival for the fittest
Happening often, even to humanity's best
To eternity, everyone falls a guest
To most a time to weep, to others a call to fest
To some they fall a jest
What lies east or west, no one's been able to tell
Same endpoint to all, the heart and lungs would arrest
But then, there remains the drama at asystole.

Rabiu Momoh

14.

Jegudujera (The Greedy One)

Long live your days, O Jegudujera
In an era of lack,
You found comfort on the people's back,
Your joy assured, as you rack up on their sufferings
Your survival ensured through their every rank and files
Frankly taking the lion's share and everything else earmarked
You live on their pain, all day long without a thank
Your ship afloat while everyone else sank
One by one, all resistance is sacked
Sac after sac, our commonwealth goes to your bank.

The visions have never been clearer
To your stronghold, everyone remains a settler,
bound by every invisible shackle and fetter.
Hard times raging, you sell a future that's never nearer
Through the cold, you're covered in an Olympic of feathers
Your growth assured, you flourish every now and later
You deny hope and their every thought of a ladder
Volume of their suffering meaning nothing,
equaling the grains in your forever living bank

Through every deed, you furthered your greed
In your every bid, the people's dream you rid
Through tricks and politics, they go without due heed
Through the magic of statistics, your gain in every feed
In the midst of plenty, they remain in need

Upon every iota of hope, you've put a lid
In every worship, your adoration have they ceded
But to the people, a seed is to be born

Out of every hood, a seed is to be born
A seed of hope and change, and the hour will come
A light would shine, darkness would understand it not
All tyranny and oppression would be set to burn
A new order and days to mourn, no more
The pain and suffering of yesteryears forever gone
There'd be joy in the city and the children would have fun in the sun
And there'd remain happiness everywhere they turn.

Rabiu Olusola Momoh

15.

Rolls Royce of a Girlfriend

Standing under the lights across the room
A symbol of grace in full bloom
Looking the best of anything begotten of a womb
Schooling everything else adorned in plume
Sending others parading beauty to gloom and doom
On this blessed night, with such pulchritude
It feels like you fell from the moon

Body chiselled out to perfect goals
Hair falling over with grace to ultimate extol
Frame carried on those long, steady legs,
The world's attention you stole
Words delivered from sensual lips,
delivered with so much soul
To your magic, we'll forever remain under control

Poised, elegant, suave and ever sassy
You excel in sophisticated finishes
Your manners are forever impeccable
Like the finest wines,
you're something of similar taste and grace
May your sweetness know no end
When you move, you twirl up a storm
Men come uneasy, wriggling like worms
Some go spilling figurative rums
A billion messages delivered from the grace of your loin
You're our unforgettable woman tonight, Joyce
You're the Rolls Royce of a girlfriend.

Rabiu Momoh

16.

O God of Creation

Songs of hope rising out of many nations
Of many languages, all to a common purpose
Of many hearts, stationed with a common desire
Young and old, all wishing for open doors
Open doors to newness of days without losses
Of sons who must daily rise with the wings of the morning
Of daughters, who must live true to beautiful essences
Of fathers, strengthening feeble hands to a common goal
Of mothers, who will unrelentingly nurture goodness and nobility
Of a people that must reach within,
honouring their journey through the times
Upon the hills, upholding justice and making manifest its visions
Through the deserts, laying testament to a better tomorrow
Across its beautiful borders, bound by peace and love
Through the forest grounds nurturing life in its diversity
Bathing its land and people with rivers of hope and equity
Harbouring plentifulness in the fields as well as in the yards
Of an Africa that must work out for its destiny
Leaving behind dark times and the many tales of woes
Of an Africa that must seek out its place with dignity and honour
Awakening to a new dawn and never resting on her oars
Till that newness of day becomes an evident reality,
In this long sail and a harrowing journey into the future,
O God of Creation, daily direct our noble cause.

17.

London City

Such is your grace, O London city!
Far and near, you receive your children while sitting pretty
You, ancient city exuding sophistication, are the pride of all counties
Through history, a beacon of hope, an amazing entity
Beautifully setting forth your children in their quests at varying
    velocities
Network of amazing buses running inter-cities
Far underground you set life in motion, something beyond crafty
Nothing spared operating the overgrounds, something very witty
A taste of you, a thrilling blend of everything fruity
Still, we won't be done singing your song, dearest London

Bless the day we marked your grounds
Your stories told in every welcoming sound
Back and forth, in their drones, your offsprings go around
In love, you opened arms to stories of all backgrounds
To everyone who finds you, a dream is found
Your love is shared in every transaction, pound for pound
Through the ages, your profound love yet abounds
Your praises sang in all corners of the earth, and yet resounds

You're built upon the grounds of healthy ambitions
Every corner of yours, a taste of beautiful action
Setting the tone for the perfect tourist attractions
Experiences taken in to full affection and ultimate satisfaction
Caring for your young and old, none falling out to faction

You land of many tales, to your sustenance we'll pay full attention
Stringing your parts stronger than any ligaments or tendons
If I ever leave, I'll be back again, dear London.

Rabiu Momoh

18.

Rite of Passage

Somewhere in the world, lays a girl in the mud
Crying hard, her little rod is gone from her pod
Gone, gone to no return and feeling very odd
Words gone from the gods, she needed to be clawed
Blood dripping, she gazed the sky for her Lord
Lord, I've been forever gored!
Gored and feeling ultimately dud
Old baba happily displaying his tool to waiting crowd
Approval nods given him, nothing confirmed with words
Bloody ratings earned, but became like a faked Ferrari

'At the right age, she must earn the rite of passage
All undue desires and rage to be controlled and locked in cage
Pluck after pluck, we'll take the petals
The filament of love to be clipped with metal
we'd arrange her flower', the sage had uttered
By ancient traditions, I was to be an addition
Or forever risk perdition and extradition
Like plough to the lawn, like a mower to the fields,
Force was required and I was cowered
Oh! What an abominable hour

Process described mildly, taking a wild turn
An unfortunate experience for the girl child, she had given thought
Her thoughts to herself, having none to confide
Like one damned, she smiled to the lie

An act perpetuated, becoming a way of life
Not entirely sure to take pride in the rite, blighted
Going through life scarred, yet well societally filed
Defiled or not, she must go on with life's ride
Hoping someday she could be the light to the unfortunate rite.

Rabiu Momoh

Excerpt from "The Drama at Asystole"

"To every man, there remains this test
The end of the survival for the fittest
Happening often, even to humanity's best
To eternity, everyone falls a guest
To most a time to weep, to others a call to fest
To some they fall a jest
What lies east or west, no one's been able to tell
Same endpoint to all, the heart and lungs would arrest
But then, there remains the drama at asystole."

19.

The Black Sheep

Music in his head, Oblak the sheep, left the fold
Against popular will, the journey began so
Each step, a moving distance away from home
Far enough for Donald, the farmer's call, to take a hold
Padded for wool, he surged happily through the cold
Joyfully in the snow, he would often fall and roll
Dutch courage, an understatement, for what makes bold
Strange joy on his face,
he hopped along like one found gold

Lost. Lost in the cold woods he was, eventually
A blind plunder through nightly conditions,
a terrible fall into the valley
Plunging far beyond imagination, no hope for a pulley
Wishing he had snapped from his folly all too early
Blackjack, Clark and Zac's help felt far hourly
Music in his head gone, clearly, he was in the deep's belly
Hungry and sore was the state of his own belly
He bleated hard to a weak fade,
hoping for a saviour from his folly
Feeling bad, sad, he sat on a pad of broken twigs
No rad of light to break the teeming gloom
Quick flashes of times happy with the lads
Crazy but lovely moments, he'd drive the flock mad
Now lost to mom, he was already lost to dad
Feeling totally outplayed by nature's card,
Oblak, the black sheep, wondered if life could be any harder

Enter Donald, the shepherd, with love and Jesus' teachings
Sacking through the woods, he went for his lost sheep
Hark, the dog, barked hard, and to the rescue he felt needed
For Donald's flock, responsibility was often truly his
Truth to tell, Oblak evokes the most possible love-hate feeling
Animal heaven joying more over one lost sheep,
Than over 99 that needed no saving
With Oblak found, the animal farm was sent to frenzy
Donald restoring the enigma in their midst.

Rabiu Momoh

20.

Eko Akete

Eko akete, Eko ilu ogbon
Right in the heart of Africa, placed like a true son
Brilliantly and your place in excellence for all days won
Through your plight, you stand right, the desire of many nations
Built upon wisdom, your wealth knows no portion
To you, many visions are born and swiftly run

Your goodness blown in with the might of the Atlantic
You stand in strength and your children make you thick
Rich in culture, you're ever vibrant and chic
Dutiful by day, at night adorned to every drop and fleek
Structure upon structure, you're laid in justice with every brick
A beacon of hope, a refuge for the strong and the weak

Exuding grace, you stand a state above all others
A gateway to goodness, far beyond many dates and orders
Through it all, you hold your inhabitants to a common fate
A promise of life and blessings beyond rates
You're blessed by the present and honoured by the lates
Showing equality, your children eat of you and are sated

You remain for many Eko akete, Eko for show
Eko ilu ogbon, Eko aromisa legbe leg be
For many years to come, may your savour persistently blow
Through your length and breadth, may riches continually sow
You are Lagos, and may your sweetness to many generations flow.

Rabiu Momoh

21.

Soldier of Fortune

A true-bred soldier, one begotten of loyalty
Awashed in love for country, a desire of all royalties
Upon shoulder once bearing an ever-enviable dignity
Devotion in your every motion, never one to be queried for dishonesty
You served the young, you served the old, all without indignity
Serving the poor, faithfully you served dignitaries
You were loved in the streets, highly regarded in countless counties

As you grew older, societal milieu got colder
The honour upon your shoulder daily getting smouldered
To truth and uprightness, you grew less and less bothered
You now answer Roger to the tune of riches
You sing Bravo to all that glitters and remains gold
You dance Tango with the big fishes without being told
To the highest bidders, you've carved a delectable niche

You became soldier to a select few and those opportuned
Flying with your goons, you garner with the biggest spoon by the
    lagoon
Calling the bluff of justice, you surf unhindered at the nation's wharf
Riding saloon around, wrecking mischiefs without impunity
You loom large with shady deals at the river of equity
Communing with likes, immunity ensured by guns and without laws
Many at your presence would begin a frantic run
We wish upon the moon that you find your heart
Bring back true honour and return our faith to where we once were

Bringing back the gallantry that once was the soldier's act
Helping to restore the soul of a nation that continually err
In unity and faith, restoring hope again in seamless art
That in your remembrance, we may but bless your memory
And in every story, your glory told without moaning.

22.

The Return to Innocence

Slowly attaining a peak and then comes the frail
While the body yet kicks, and then it slowly bail
Hail the all-achieving human, and then senility starts to unveil
Like nail driven through bones, the body progressively weaken
The flying mind loses its ways and whatever makes it tick
At the nick of time, there's a sure return to innocence

The slow but sure return of the body to innocence,
Process begun not to be altered by any incense
By denial or alteration, a process that denies all pretence
Including all who sit on the fence
Or act out in full defence
Offence remains unintended
From thence, nature shows to be master of all

To even the bold, the story is foretold
For all the gold gathered, the body starts to get old
Old and unable to bear a cold
Cold and ever desiring a fold
Life's truth is told
and man feels bought and sold

A new age is begun as man loses his runs
New pages of life desired but never to be turned
The stage performances left to those yet to come undone
The mind left in its cage, as the sun goes down
All plumage lost and the body worn
No pun intended as the body returns to innocence.

Rabiu Momoh

23.

Temiloluwa

Dear Temiloluwa,
In the garden of life, I birthed a flower
One to love and cherish for many, many hours
Gift to mankind and a blessing to this sower
Amidst many who hover,
you'll find my love like no other
Each day it gets newer and ever tall like a tower

You'll find the sun and its people so good
The richness of the earth and the oceans so blue
Lovely relatives and friends so true
Stick to love and positivity in your heart daily renewed
The brightness of the mornings and beginnings so new
Love all at most, and even the 1% few

Li'l one, you'll find many truths in my sayings
Sometimes you'll find love, other times you'd be left waiting
Find strength in my company, other times you'd be praying
For those nights, your mind should find training
For all the best things in the world, I hope you find gainings
Sometimes you'll win, sometimes you'd be left trying
It remains to say that for most days you should be flying

When all's been said and done,
True to my love, you'll never go wrong
Through the long life's journey, we'll remain as one

Find strength and comfort here, as well as in your mom
Greatness and grace for many days would be forever yours
For through this strong loin, you were brought forth.

Rabiu Momoh

24.

Under the Same Sky

Sigh.
And we are all under the same sky
The Thais, the Masais, the Samurais and those in Shanghai
From the wonderful skylines of Philadelphia
Down to the arid planes of the Sahara
To one a moment to born, to another a moment to die
The young man beholding the beauty in his lover's eyes
The little one lulling off to sweet lullabies
The many trading places, items to buy
From the blacks to the whites,
and all the glorious colours in-between
The unity in our diversity none can deny

The claims and the counterclaims
To many, it all feels like a game
Make a name or go forever lame
See well to your aims and you might find fame
Acclaimed enough to take a dame by the Thames
Name cheered to loud exclaim
See to a scandal and go really defamed
Thin line between being aflame and getting maimed
Above all, we're one and the same

Renting the open sky is the thunder
A man's sorrows comforted by another, the bartender
Nothing to erase his many blunders

The long rain hours remain a ruse to the builder
Children dancing in the rain, amazed by nature's wonder
To the lovers on the night, the rain makes it all fonder
That the farmer is the best benefactor, to that there's no contender
Through the chaos, to the man in space, the earth looks in order
And we're all under the same sky

From the cheerful coastlines of the Brasilia
Through the welcoming arms of the Canadians
Fall for the beautiful optimism of the child in Africa
Explore the sunny conditions of Australia
And the amazing deep-rooted cultures of the Asians
The absorbing love for football among the Europeans
It stands true we all belong to one race
And that is the human race
Love is the answer
'Cos we're all under the same sky.

Rabiu Momoh

Excerpt from the poem "Eko Akete"

"Exuding grace, you stand a state above all others
A gateway to goodness, far beyond many dates and orders
Through it all, you hold your inhabitants to a common fate
A promise of life and blessings beyond rates
You're blessed by the present and honoured by the lates
Showing equality, your children eat of you and are sated

You remain for many Eko akete, Eko for show
Eko ilu ogbon, Eko aromisa legbe legbe
For many years to come, may your savour persistently blow
Through your length and breadth, may riches continually sow
You are Lagos, and may your sweetness to many generations flow"

25.

Rage of Delusions

Far beyond our galaxy the warships gather
Gathering in might at the call of their leader
Freida and Jedda ensuring every order at the call of Zedda
On earth, an age of machines to declare on her
The solar system and its beings to take over
A galaxy run by men who believe in life in no other

Far from this gathering and down here in every hood,
the mood is good, and life is what everyone exudes
Plenty of food and in happiness everyone stood
From arid regions, to the oceans and deep into the woods,
upon the Armageddon to come, no one did brood
To life in its continuity everyone alludes
Barring this lone man to whom everything deludes

Signals received in their torrents, my head bearing a hose
A call to prepare from coast to coast is what I haste to toast
Send words and letters out to everyone across all coasts
Man every high point and leave none without a post
Step down from your high thoughts and all grandiosed
Time to bare spaceship and rockets to which you make boast
and leave none to arms to say the most

Hear O father, hear O son
Smear the tears off O daughter, 'cause the end may be near
Remove all fears and your war gears do wear

A call to bear arms, to even the very queer
The young man soon to part from his very beer
And maybe we can fight the offensives off in the end

But wait, the thoughts rage in my head like one stalked
Notions and assumptions played out and the many talks
Talks of doom and gloom, deep in my head locked
Putting in a sense of urgency to it and a ticking clock
Bulk of ideas streaming in, flight of ideas in a flock
Sometimes they feast, feasting on my mind with their forks

I remain the one by the block you dock from
Flock after flock, you pass me by like clockwork
I remain rooted to the grounds with the company of my thoughts
Sun-up to sun-down, I live with every silent mocks
Knocked down to earth, I feel locked out from heaven
I am Caesar and with me no evil lurks.

Rabiu Momoh

26.

A Bull in a China Shop

Out at noon goes an amazing look
A hungry bull led by a happy fool
A fool at noon, feeling forever cool
Step after step, they hopped like they bore rule
Songs in head, having onlookers for a pool
Over people's eyes they pulled a wool
Wetted by the drool from the mouth of the bull

Off they went, headed for the china shop
A gentle afternoon headed for a giant flop
Flop beyond the save of any watchful cop
Fate untold, they made it past the diner and every stop
China man and Nina, sinners at one thought
Fina and Vina onlookers as things took a turn

House of saucers came crashing without a buzzer
Matter of concern for any Snapchat and Twitter
Cups, plates and spoons were up for no watchers
Up in the air and everywhere, as things splattered
Right in the china shop, the bull became a winner
On empty belly, a winner in a mystery fight by all concerns.

27.

Made of Black

From the sunny sides of the world came these overcomers
Human variants made tough under the hammer of the sun
To strength and in-built resilience, they were surely no comers
To their chequered history and its acceptance,
they played no undercovers
The long and tortuous journey birthed Obama, Luther, Mandela and
    Soyinka
and there remains the fantastic spirit of black in Africa

Cross the times and their many experiences,
they've become truly made
Made of grace, made of hope,
on bed of forgiveness forever laid
Made of light and shine, blending dark in lovely shades
Some of hers have found their foot,
others still requiring aids
There remains to them a future,
a future whose due they mustn't evade
A due of commitment to excellence and life till all else fades

Now and forever, the spirit of Africa would have your back
Wake up each day, bear solutions to your people's lack
For progressiveness and for joy ultimately,
please always have a knack
Knowing every day may not always be a walk in the park

There remain these tasks O African sons,
and they forever come in sacs
When all's been said and done,
there remains a fantastic spirit of black in Africa.

Rabiu Olusola Momoh

28.

Tears of the Sun

Millions of miles away, I stay drenched in tears
My sorrow about little earth, for which I daily care
Tears of suffering souls all so audible, it feels so near
Light years away, like a magnet, your pain I bear
The next odd thing to happen remains a palpable fear
Please give a reason to hope again, my dear little earth

What lays naked before my eyes perpetually stun
Brothers sworn in deceit under the watching sun
Brittle peace maintained, hands ready with guns
To forbearance, many would begin a run
A run against the humanity, sadly happy to see things burn
Please take me back to your faded memories, my dear little earth

Your contagious confusion, like a mail, I daily get
Many a soul would fret, outside many doors lay nets
Nets you'll bet leading many to a proverbial death
A death to conscience and goodwill, in disregard daily set
To the few good men, your dearth worries me at length
Please find hope and strength, however little you have left

Alone here in your outer space I sing my song
Songs of sorrow, of little earth that could once do no wrong
A tune to remind her each one, to everyone belongs
That the cord of brotherhood to infinity, forever binds all
Touching the earth and touching me, the feeling is so long
I am the sun, your jewel in the sky,
for ages to come we'll be as one.

Rabiu Olusola Momoh

29.

Grandiose

Upon the blue waters, posing by fleet of luxury boats
Endless flow of incomes, adorning designer coats
Intercontinental dishes, enough to make a man bloat
Lovely oats out of China and meals out of the finest goats
Mansions by the sea, properties in different area codes
My words in gold, money speaking, best quoted drinking

I bet you see me in your vivid dreams
Preen and proper, adorned to the finest trim
Suave, confidence full and flowing off the brim
Wisdom at its height, a figure far beyond flimsy
Nursed by your models, catered by your every best team
I am every dream, and for all days my glory would beam

Parties so lavish, Jacuzzis, and all wears on Versace
Good on every look, happy children in every nook
World powers on my call, waiting in line, my fall to stall
From world's end travel my trucks of gold,
don't act like you've never been told.
Gardens by many streams, I remain your every dream.

Rabiu Olusola Momoh

30.

Obeisance

Far from France, enter an unexpected journey
Like one in trance, a drift of fate to our emperor's party
An unwelcomed guest, wearing nothing to be fancied
Nothing fanciful, not even worth a repeat glance
Princes at supper, dressed dapper, citizens afar as onlookers
Onlookers, not once, not deserving of the table served
Bloopers at game, creating fun at nothing proper
Wining and dining right into the dead of the night
Fine wine from Nice in France and cheer ultimate delight
Perhaps not the night to give the princess out outrightly
Enters the Emperor's riddle at the dead of the night
A taste of something nice, a source describing its niceness
Worthy princes took a fail, the emperor opined
Save an unknown figure, a taste all so known
He did the obeisance and gave Nancy her first dance.

Rabiu Olusola Momoh

Excerpt from "Made of Black"

"Now and forever,
the spirit of Africa would have your back
Wake up each day, bear solutions to your people's lack
For progressiveness and for joy ultimately,
please always have a knack
Knowing every day may not always be a walk in the park
There remain these tasks O African sons,
and they forever come in sacs
When all's been said and done,
there remains a fantastic spirit of black in Africa"

Rabiu Olusola Momoh

31.

Medical Cannabinoids

A taste of her,
A taste of life
A taste of high,
A taste of fly
Doing cloud nine
Joy that's all mine
Joy blended out in cookies
All the gladness for this rookie
A taste of tipped fine wine
or that magical chew for life
Goodness in a cloud of vapour
Oil of gladness under tongue to pour
God bless this magical America
Medical THC is all mine
About something publicly bad,
 I ultimately feel really glad
In the end, this might hurt
But surely this cancer does more?

Rabiu Olusola Momoh

32.

The Illusion

Far in the distance, a vision of hope
Through life's desert, a sight begging devotion
Many who wouldn't cope are stationed to its present dryness
Its quotation unto achievement requiring dutiful intentions
Many caught deluded given little room unto correction
With willful decisions standing the ultimate solution,
and the promotion closer begging all due attention,
the journey to a future in illusion creates our today's realities.
Otherwise, the present dryness remains the ready connection.

Rabiu Olusola Momoh

33.

Horsepower

A sweet glow in the dark at the thought of its flower
A slow-but-sure mount, albeit to full power
Manpower made ever ready for its golden hour
Nature's wonder, daring in might like a tower
Sustaining life for ages long, the ultimate sower
From welcoming Dover to sweet Virginia,
you find strength and guise like Bauer in Philadelphia
In the face of many fights, surely never one to cower

Through the ages, fighting humanity's cause
Built to strength, something in the might of a horse
At height of activity, exuding life's sauce without a fuss
Flossed here, tossed there, you find safety within a purse
A ready tool, a source of an ever-pleasurable height
Elixir and life in the fluid that you hold bank
Flanked by your generals, designed to get sank
Shooting for the stars, never one to fire blank
At full attention, flying at half-mast or lying like a plank,
barring any alluded pranks,
many today hold you in ultimate thanks.

Rabiu Momoh

34.

Fruit of the Womb

Tick after tick, the new month looms
The long wait, the fate of this beauty in full bloom
Waiting, waiting for this plume to bear an essence
They tarry to bear seeds in its waiting room
Vessel ashore, tender ones to carry
Feeling the gloom created by vessel watchers,
She wished upon the moon for the fruit of the womb

Month after month, the red ship remained ashore
Ashore long enough, as the seaweeds gathered
By the month, shedding off in red effluents
In and out goes the Lord of the rods,
With each mount, shedding off happy contents
In and out to ensure beloved ship is fed and sated
Waiting for contents to sail north to joyous reception

At the fullness of time, a dream is born
Bringing joy like the sun in winter
Something all so tender and so mild, a son or daughter
To you, we've been for all days assigned
Sitting snugly by the breast,
our hopes and stars are forever aligned.

Rabiu Momoh

35.

The Bucket List

What it'd take to fulfill a long daring list
For many acts, one to act out the beast
The beast. The beast who'd insist and persist
Resisting every inertia to ever get started
Fulfilling all that many would rather gist about
Amidst many fears, feasting on many wishes
The bucket list to achieve, to ever say the least

Out of the skies, taking a dive like Obama
Or take a chill by the blissful Christ the Redeemer
Doing the long walk on the Great Wall of China
Or do a hang over the Leaning Tower of Pisa
To go scuba diving to the oceans deep
Living out many nights over the skylines of Dubai
Life would surely be a thrill, and I'd love to buy

To these endeavours, the tickets remain within
To live out inner pleasures, surely playing no puppets
Making out purchases off the marketplaces of impossibilities
The limiting power of budget ever needing to be at bay
To have every gut to pull wishes from pockets
To be off the hook, like one out of every holding socket
Would be to have ticked off wishes off the bucket list
To the many power nights with the Queen
Sitting right next to Bill Gates and Obama

To explore many fun nights out in Ibiza,
while still doing the many goods I can
To have lived out the blessedness of nature in Bali
I surely would have lived out many bucket lists.

Rabiu Momoh

Excerpt from "Fruit of The Womb"
"At the fullness of time, a dream is born
Bringing joy like the sun in winter
Something all so tender and so mild, a son or daughter
To you, we've been for all days assigned
Sitting snugly by the breast,
our hopes and stars are forever aligned."

Rabiu Momoh

Excerpt from "Greatest of All Times"

"I am every legend
Sing my praises times without end
Knock out all who stand but pretend
Tell my tales in every land and beyond
To the ones unborn, my legend please attend
I'll forever be in every heart
Because I'm your greatest of all times"

Rabiu Momoh

36.

ERU

Ships from across the many seas seeking men who are able
Able souls to work the stables
Why not? When truly found capable
Ade, Tade, Lade and Imade
Men standing in strength as a bull
With unyielding stubbornness worse than a mule
Give them tools to work our lands that are arable
When of course, they are Erus.

Standing there in skin made over by the tropical sun
Fathers, mothers, daughters, and sons
Going different ways to gainful auditions
Sometimes a-seat to hurtful renditions
Strokes and blows like one to perdition

Hands bound, feet in fetters
Body broken, mind and will in shatters
Nothing but leather patches to cover my manners
By laws and letters, I'm bound to my master
I'll obey my mistress, nothing must upset her
Li'l master eats his butter while I work the gutters
Of course, I know my place, 'cos I'm an Eru.

Ample years passed, over our freedom we bore no rule
Skin hatched out in latches to no ridicule
Hands callused out, bearing testament to work tools

We worked the castles and tendered the cattle
Brothers and sisters still crossing the waters in bundles
The indirect rule to ensure every move
Less cool for school, but found a book for the soul
When truly, I was an Eru.

37.

G.O.A.T

Consider the times one end to another
Search all too hard, and you'll find no other
From forefathers to godfathers,
after me you'll go no further
Brothers went hard, but often would stutter
What I'm made of, just don't bother
Across the various climes,
I remain the greatest of all times

I remain far above every jest
Leading all quests, so none can contest
Far from the east, all down to the west
I'm honoured more than your crests can tell
Day after day, I put the limits to the test
There remains me and the fall of the rest
Through all the sweats and zests,
I'm worth your celebrations and fests
Across all that looks sublime,
I stand the greatest of all times

From one to every other victory dance,
I'll forever stand in your remembrance
Smashing the records and out-smarting all in attendance
With my golds breaking out every balance,
You can tell all that I am in one glance
Donning all that glitters,
I've been your greatest of all times

I am every legend
Sing my praises times without end
Knock out all who stand but pretend
Tell my tales in every land and beyond
To the ones unborn, my legend please attend
I'll forever be in every heart
Because I'm your greatest of all times.

Rabiu Momoh

38.

Butterfly Kelly

Leisurely flew Kelly, the pride of the garden
Zig here, zag there, all without a worry
Blessing nature with matchless colours adorned,
Your beauty rate tops and next to none
Such grace in the flaps of your wings,
pleasant thrills remain all that you bring
Guided by lovingly attached antennas,
regal in your beautiful manners,
you bless rich flowers with your ever chic and style

Landing on rich petals without a stigma,
the next 7-star nectar all to gather
With every sip, Kelly feeds her belly
Having no need for loverboy Nelly
You glean, glean, glean and then leave,
leaving your donors with such a honour,
Honours taken and no strings attached

Kelly,
to me, you remain a stunner of a lady
Thoughts of you make my heart flutter
I'm sometimes lovestoned, with nothing to utter
When you leave, all I have is love litters
Enough to make me stutter and sometimes flustered
My petals need your love every time on a platter, Kelly
To mine, please be a settler
Find in me nectar and love so true
All day together till we both wither.

Rabiu Momoh

39.

The Black Reference

On a matter I wouldn't love to sit on a fence,
Thanks for asking me for a reference, O Employer!
For me to write about Vince, that remains an unforgivable error,
Surely something close to travesty
To write would be to paint a black pot heavenly white
Changing dishonesty to honesty with the strokes of a pen
I wouldn't play to his defence,
surely not after all his offences
In the end, I wouldn't have written based on inferences
But with due reverence, I'd have written about his lack of deference
Ultimately leading to our severance and many dirty dances
Severance away from my league of very cultured workers

I bet what you see is not what you'll get
Hence making it hard for me to vet
Expecting something to pet and groom,
we were soon met with a wolf
A wolf in sheep or human clothing at best
Jet speed should be how you run from him
He remains a damaged good, damaged with all-time effects
Damaged, ever-damaged beyond any possible reset
In all effects, his coworkers surely stand bound to be affected

Dutiful he wrote he was, but fell short of pitiful to me
For focus, he was a locus of distraction
Vince, like his friend Mark, couldn't make up for every lack

Both having a knack to rack up inquiries
Going around in their own bubble,
they give anyone double for their troubles
Every tete-a-tete ended like a quest,
I storm away on wobbly knees

He's, however, a bright chap
Dig him deep enough you'd make an excellent tap
Who'd someday earn a feather to cap
He's a scattered goody, needing wrap up
Every dog sure has his day
Hoping, someday, his greatness would see the light of day
To take or not to take?
Decision would remain forever yours, dear employer
For me, I've lived my days
And I was a taker.

40.

Obama

You rolled out to audiences in no regular clichés
Speeches you made fit for all times
For all times, you delivered without itches
Pitch after pitch, for 8 years you lulled your opponents
Nicely done, all without screeches
Nothing accidental, you stood monumental
Of African roots, all so presidential

You were like a dream,
a dream whose time did come
Among many men, you stood prime
Across many climes, you stood sublime
A symbol of light and ultimate delight
For you the stars did align,
and you made the paradigms shift.

Dr Rabiu Momoh

Excerpt from "Obama"
"You were like a dream,
a dream whose time did come
Among many men, you stood in prime
Across many climes, you stood sublime
A symbol of light and ultimate delight
For you the stars did align,
and you made the paradigms shift."

Rabiu Momoh

41.

The One That Got Away

Out here in your city, by the bay
Heart goes out to the one that got away
Away, that fateful May you went away, Kay
Nothing. Nothing left of our love, not even a ray
How by the watersides we would lay on the hay
The promise of your love you'd often say
Lovely songs would go out from your music box,
far in the distance, your mule would bray
Food in hands, heart served out in trays
How all your fears, I'd allay,
Promising and cheering how we'd stay for all days
nothing standing in our way
Your sweet self, never the one to pay lip service,
human as clay, the May you left, and everything changed

Slowly. Very slowly, I lost you, never expecting the plot
Like water spilling from a boiling pot, our love was soon gone
The glut of your affection was lost to hurtful lots
Distance threw in the rot, and we got sorely caught
Putting a knife to the knot that binds our love
Like the morning dew, you were soon gone
A figment of memory, of some sort, never to be retouched
A dot in history never to be re-enacted
I sought and fought for what was ours
But you were truly far gone

Hart should know he won the race for your love
That you're the one someone always wanted
Many days, dusk to dawn, I was undone
Feeling the tension of your departure, I did mourn
Our burning love never to be fawned over
Many daughters did excellently, none came close to you
I found Joanne and life began again
The sun of love rose to full shone again
Joanne knows this love story
Someday you'd meet Shaun and Gareth, my sons
Never tell them you're the one that got away.

Rabiu Momoh

42.

The Preacher

The voice of him crying out upon the hills
Out in the streets, and into the night still
Calling for ransom of souls, not requiring a bill
Souls the eternal enemy seeks for a kill
Before a kill, reducing to a nil
Before nil, their many virtues to steal
Before virtues stolen, contemplations in their heart to fill
Li'l by li'l, men of will left with no clean bill

The story of man's perpetual fall he'd shout and tell
The stories of his glory and how from grace he fell
How many years ago, humanity's cat had been belled
The restoration formulary to man again to sell
Divinity and eternity in humanity's heart to forever well again
Between man and his maker, the veil of divide to take away

The cattle upon the thousand hill is the Lord's
Those were the words of a man with a burden for God
To redeem a generation and the enemy's gored
Seeking a ransom for those already bought by blood
To get the rods off the back of a people by his words
To restore the people's savour and those divinely bored
Like a plant in the spring, hoping man could bud again.

Rabiu Momoh

43.

Evergreen

In a moment, and like a gentle blow of a breeze
Life as we know, and then it ceases to be
To some, a sweet nod of approval,
a soul that pleases and Jeez! it ceases,
to others a daring moment to take a hiss
To the young or old, the endless cold blows
Holding a-freeze any further seed to sow
Even to the best of humans, the heaviest blow is dealt
To the best prepared, the coldest loss is felt
The ever-watchful eyes bow out, losing its glow
Man's guard lets down and then he forever takes a bow

The once still river of life runs out,
Out and faster than the thought of a doubt
The stout and tout left with one less to flout
Death deals with the biggest hand,
a rout and a bout like never before seen
The clock ticks out; out and about on the saint
On the saint, as well as on the soul that sins
Man's life is recounted like one who paints

From New York to Yorkshire,
Man's luck runs out and he ultimately retires
An end to all that sustains a life fully wired
The clock strikes its last and a soul takes a dive
A dive for one deprived or the one who jives
An end to a transaction of life and all that makes alive
and death, by grand design, claims the best buyer.

Rabiu Olusola Momoh

44.

A million shades of lovely

You were like a night of many stars,
a vision all so desirable
You gave your love, we stood in awe,
one all so amiable
You stood like a rock, all round the clock,
all day very bankable
A wife to one, a sweetheart of many millions,
from your love, we were inescapable
A figure of hope, soul sister so dope,
our dear first lady, all so able
Many came in their grades and shades,
you stood many miles beyond compare
and for many days, lovingly attributable.
Humbly giving true vibes,
you made affection truly accessible.
You are our million shades of lovely
You're Michelle, an angel of grace,
for all days giving love from core to shell.

Rabiu Olusola Momoh

45.

Rainbow Workforce

Out of many nations,
far and near, bearing representations
Of many languages and tongues,
of varying backgrounds and experiences,
to man many stations,
across many days
and through many long nights
across many area codes
through many lands and spaces
a rainbow of forces,
a blend of purpose and expressions
from the best of sons and daughters
your cause to achieve
albeit very effectively
Your praises sung
Vision ensured
Goals achieved
Truly because they can.

Rabiu Olusola Momoh

46.

The Animal Farm

I long for those stories from the old Pa Animashaun's farm
Those endless tales of our lives told in harmless riddles
How the hen should not glory all too much in its beautiful feathers
Because someday, they'll bear a lesser import than the meat it serves
The crow of the cock upon the clock mocking Hublot's timepiece
How sometimes the beautiful things of life may go to the un-deserving,
our endless wonder with a gold ring in the snout of Tameka the Pig
The majesty of Stallone the Stallion, yet he ain't the king of animals
Those long thoughtful look on the face of Ruckie the Duck,
like she holds all of the world's truth in a firm lock,
truths told in her humble walk of her duckling all in a file
The strange-but-true stories in the eyes of the cow,
who have journeyed far from the country's north,
serving goodness out in milk, meat, hides and bones
The sense of duty in the face of Danny the Dog
The unfailing routine of Clark the Cock to crow
Your urging voice welcoming the farm to a new day
The horses neigh endlessly, the pig bleats
The hen cackles while the turkey clucks
While the enemy mocks and forever lurk,
there's yet life within Pa Animashaun's farm.

Rabiu Momoh

47.

The Night Shift

Little by little, creeping upon the waiting man was the night
Day so good, hoping the night would be so right
He thought loudly, height of work shouldn't feel like a fight
More than feeling like a fight, definitely not a plight
Staying through the hours, the clock mocked ever gleefully
At every corner, work lurked, with nowhere to dock
Blocks of work pushed out, till feelings became stone-cold
Stone-cold feeling to work the very stone-cold nights
By morning comes the unwelcomed burnout
The slow burnout while end-products were turned out
Body ripped to tiredness on a job he felt wired out for
The drive home for another day, the bus all the better
Landing on his bed and then he tapped out.

Rabiu Olusola Momoh

Excerpt from "The Return to Innocence"

"A new age is begun as man loses his runs
New pages of life desired but never to be turned
The stage performances left to those yet to come undone
The mind left in its cage, as the sun goes down
All plumage lost and the body worn
No pun intended as the body returns to innocence"

Rabiu Momoh

48.

The Misfits

In a country in dire search for her soul
Her best needs would be leaders to make her whole
Not some square pegs in her many round holes
To take her from a plunge into an eternal hole
Leaders, and not bidders who have sworn deceitfully
Leaders who have not lifted souls to vanity
Helpers of her destiny to forever play feeders
Leaders to go from merely speaking to laying true credence
Setting her visions aright without an iota of pretence
Leaders to ensure her ideals by all and sundry
Her ideals as far as her cause is found
Bound, bound, by faith, unity, equality and goodwill
Pound for pound, goodness in her every sound
Till the unity of faith shed astounding love around.

Rabiu Olusola Momoh

49.

Iyaniwura (Mother is Golden)

In the creator's eyes, one born out of cheer necessity
To a failing man, a figure of ultimate prosperity
An instrument of love, a helper of immense capacity
One with love so unrepenting, even through all adversities
One to know, love and hold for days, knowing no duplicity
Surely not one to hold back, your magnanimity known to all eternity

Through the ages old, our lives you bore and steered
Through the cold, you help us have no fear
Your dreams often sold off for the ones you rear
Holding steadfastly, you show your every love and care
Through rough and tough times, you spare nothing from your   fold
An ornament of grace, you're divinity in human mould

There remains this fount of grace in every mother
Shedding love so true and yet abounds for many days
A well of prayers to surmount every mount and high places
Loyal to every call, one to count on to displace all odds
Known for order and one far from betrayal
You're golden, mother,
truly one like no other.

Rabiu Olusola Momoh

50.

70% (Water)

It remains to say that water is life
The truth upon which many things thrive
Sustaining life and processes all without a strive
From Kent to Kentucky, and all the way to Maldives,
with love and purity, you ensure many happy vibes
Many who are happy would take a dive,
the young and the old, and the lovely housewife

From cradle to the grave, you find a use
Through the hustles and bustles, many lives you save
To Dave and to many who crave,
to the feeble and ultimately to the brave,
to those by candlelit nights and those in faraway caves,
to those burdened with care and to those who rave,
to the many sages and the few depraved,
to the kids jumping in muddy puddles,
most of life's essence you ultimately save.

O the might of every living waters,
Good for Willow, also good for Walter
All through the ages, your destiny unaltered
Through many rocks, you stand a gentle cutter
By many coasts, your voice stays a soothing mutter
Honour to you O gentle element, plotter of many destinies

Over the earth surface, you cover 70%
Blessing life and nature, not charging a cent
Sustaining those who come, and those who are sent
Bless the beautiful ladies and our many handsome gents
Bless those in the fields, bless those in tents
Bless the landowners, bless those who rent
Bless those who feast, bless those in Lent
The might of your powers, please never vent
You are our living waters; you are our life.

Rabiu Olusola Momoh

51.

The Perfect Storm

Perfect night predicted, everyone loving the news
The storm grew leaving all without a clue
Blowing hard and fast, our losses we're left to rue
Joyful memories fast gone, sadness was left in lieu
Like axe to tree, our ship of life was left for the hew
All lights gone, the moon cast vision in dark hues

Memories of blissful times and how nicely we'd forage
Here and there your thoughts came while the wild storm continues to rage
Those ages seeming far, now turned on is this page of darkness
Wild thoughts of past sins, its visiting wages upon the sea staged
On a happy night, the devil was let out of its cage
Arranging his plot on us, all sadly without a gauge

Lovely evening cheers replaced by absolute fear
Men in suits and ladies in perfect gears
Clutching on boards, not knowing how we'd fare
Many drowned in thoughts, with no beer to clear the air
Life slowly drifting, doom and gloom in clear stare
Cries of all intensities, many unto a saviour's dare

Through the long and cold night, few stood believing
Wave after wave, the storm's intensity slowly abating
At the glimpse of sun, peace and still came with its turning
Freeing those who stood against the night's goings
The stormy nights are far gone and a new day dawning
The slow drift ashore and a faint cheer to new beginnings.

Rabiu Olusola Momoh

52.

Show of shame

Out in the streets, victim of a lame game
Strutting along mindlessly, tailors to no blame
A figure so regal, played in a show of shame
Caught by young men and beautiful dames alike
An act for a day, bearing an eternal flame

Shame so measured, fit for an emperor's frame
Tamed, each day after never to remain the same
Aiming for fame, pity was served to wide acclaim
A respectable image cut in a slur of names
A story for all days, a royalty's image stood maimed.

Rabiu Olusola Momoh

Excerpt from "Gone"

"And so, I ran
As fast in life as my feet could carry me
Running that lane that was meant for me
Daring to attain heights I was meant to be
For me to see, feel and to be became the deal
Finding the lead inside me was the greater deal
Paying the world in its own bill
While running my race, you were far gone
Like the bullet out of a shotgun, you were truly far gone"

Rabiu Momoh

53.

The Serpent

Slowly through the garden, the serpent would go
High and low, plain grounds and through many furrows
Lying, swerving and prying, you sowed a seed
Shedding guile around, the next corruption to sow
A seed unto damnation and man's life became borrowed

To creatures gullible, the next reality blow to dole
To those vowed to light, the next shadow of deceit to cast
The queen of stealth, you spew your venom and many follow
The mystery behind that famous tree, we don't seek to know
But rather too late, man took the fall like one to the gallows

Your seed of sin sown, many today still wallow
Wallowing fast and deep, the ways of corruption to tow
Among the cast-outs, man became a chief fellow
The chief fellow on a redemption path so narrow
Leaving man down and forever seeking to fill a hollow.

Rabiu Olusola Momoh

54.

The Enigma of England

There remain the existing wonders of England
The height of structures and functions and land of beautiful brands
World orders rose and fell, you took steady civilization ready at hand
Land of bright lights and beauty in your every spark
Your sights and sounds to the corners of the earth, without a brag
Many a man, to your dream, would begin a run
A run to fun and goodness of utmost intentions
A land of willful decisions and precisions in appreciation
Bound by protocols and guidelines, you eschew excellence bottom-line
Highlighting progress, you're a marker of fairness underlined
Rich in culture and forever preserving history
Your glory told in ever-perpetuated fanciful stories
You took your falls and built a land for all
You're England and the glory of all lands.

Rabiu Olusola Momoh

55.

Rat Race

Day after day, like clockwork, I'm worked
Sunrise to sunset, my commute with people in flocks
Hours and after-hours, to this paid routine I'm stuck
Some days are fairly easy, others are as hard as rock
Knock after knock, I'll hang in there for more bucks
Pluck after pluck, I'd work at the dock

Some believing in long hours, others wishing upon luck
Some working off their gloves, others pulling off their socks
To some businesses open, others their doors to lock
Some playing fair, others for gullible customers they lurk
Some a-seat while money comes, others their portion is to hawk
Surely with hard work comes wealth,
while health is slowly taken away with a fork

In this life, there remains a race
Some dashing fast, others are slow in their ways
A race in time and space, albeit for many days
Some just to get by, others their race to ace
The ultimate race for money and all it can lace
Finding human wants insatiable,
and that remains the ultimate daze.

Rabiu Olusola Momoh

56.

Life ecclesiastical

From the very first breath,
down to its very last,
life in itself happens to all.
The many choices already for one
The few decided ones of great importance
The run at the break of each of day
The short nights, its longer stay we'd pray
To the many friends who leave their marks and go
To the many hurts wrought, but the heart would go on
From many cheerful moments in celebration,
to times head lowered in hurtful mourning
The joy of many unions,
to the pain of hurtful separations
From the joy of welcoming newborn,
to watching them leave as adults.
From many moments of arrivals and departures,
to the many moments of sleeping and waking up,
life throws in all its mixes.
The ups, the downs and everything in-between
When life's final breath is to be drawn,
Life, in itself, would have happened to all.

Rabiu Olusola Momoh

57.

Gone

And so it began
Floods of life-changing decisions that had to be made
When the gentleman matured to really needing a maid
Times it blew hot to really needing shade
Life's lessons cutting through deeper than a blade
Days it all seems like it's about who had the biggest raid
And the world limited in its capacity to aid
Like a candlelight out in the rain
You were gone too soon

And there were times
Efforts made just wouldn't seem to rhyme
Christmas bells for us wouldn't chime
When it truly felt more acidic than lime
When everyone's Mercedes really felt bigger than mine
Like salt meeting water,
You were gone pretty too soon

Then I began to plan
When it's all I must do to be the man
Keeping the freshness of my dreams from the sun's tan
Daily getting my schemes out of the can

The man, his can and the times needing to be in tandem
Daring to don my successes like a royal diadem
Like the comet out in the night sky
You were gone all too soon

And so I ran
As fast in life as my feet could carry me
Running that lane that was meant for me
Daring to attain heights I was meant to be
For me to see, feel and to be became the deal
Finding the lead inside me was the greater deal
Paying the world in its own bill
While running my race, you were far gone
Like the bullet out of a shotgun, you were truly far gone.

Rabiu Olusola Momoh

CPSIA information can be obtained
at www.ICGtesting.com
Printed in the USA
BVHW042104191020
591325BV00003BA/1071